Mothers Are Wonderful

MOTHERS ARE WONDERFUL

Warm Words of Praise by Pat Boone,
Pearl Bailey, Margaret Mead,
Billy Graham and many more

Selected by Lois Huffmon Hunt

Illustrated by Ginny Cresswell

Hallmark Editions

MOTHERS ARE WONDERFUL

Beauty is expression.
When I paint a mother
I try to render her beautiful
by the mere look
she gives her child.

Jean Francois Millet

Young Mother

She holds him in her arms
      And murmurs lullabies;
While all the hope
      of motherhood
      Is shining in her eyes.

His eyes are pools that mirror
      Her dreams, her joys,
      her fears;
And in their depths is hidden
      The wonder of the years.

Kay Wissinger

Only One Mother

Most of all
the other beautiful things
in life come by twos and threes,
by dozens and hundreds.
Plenty of roses,
stars, sunsets, rainbows,
brothers and sisters,
aunts and cousins,
but only one mother
in the whole world.

Kate Douglas Wiggin

Mothers' arms are made
of tenderness,
and sweet sleep blesses
the child who lies therein.

Victor Hugo

A mother is put together
of wondrous things --
soft hands to caress
a tired head,
firm fingers to guide
a growing child
along the right path,
and a warm breast
to shield her little one
against the world.

Wanda Beal

My mother…had no career;
but she had a character,
and it was of a fine
and striking and lovable sort….
She had a slender,
small body but a large heart--
a heart so large
that everybody's grief
and everybody's joys
found welcome in it…
she felt a strong interest
in the whole world
and everything
and everybody in it….

Mark Twain

…My memory of her
is of someone always marvelously
fresh and pretty,
although when I examine it
I see that
she wore the same dresses
year after year.
But she could twist
a ribbon in such a way
or so pin a flower
at her throat
that she looked as though
she wore a new gown.

Pearl S. Buck

Mother's love grows by giving.

Charles Lamb

Home to me is laughter,
     kisses on the cheek,
          warm looks and tender touches
               when the heart's too full
                    to speak.
Home is sharing happiness
     and dreams I'm dreaming of--
Home to me is Mother,
Home to me is love.

Mary Loberg

My mother and I
have a special relationship.
We have an agreement
that I can tell her my problems
as I would tell a friend,
and she will give advice
from a friend's standpoint....
I admire my mother
more than anyone
in the world.

Lynda Robb

Definition

Mother--A word that holds
    the tender spell
Of the dear
    essential things of earth;
A home, clean sunlit rooms,
        and the good smell
Of bread, a table spread,
    a glowing hearth.
And love beyond the dream
    of anyone...
I search for words for her...
    and there are none.

Grace Noll Crowell

A mother laughs our laughter,
Sheds our tears,
Returns our love,
Fears our fears.
She lives our joys,
Cares our cares,
And all our hopes and dreams
she shares.

Julia Summers

Who ran to help me when I fell
    and would some pretty story tell
    or kiss the place to make it well?
My mother.

Ann Taylor

17

When... The oatmeal is finished
      And wiped off their faces,
      The boxes of lunches
      Are snatched from their places,
      The sound of the school bus
      Makes feet fly and scurry,
      And Mother is kissed
      (Or missed) in the hurry,
Then... I reheat the coffee
      And fill up my cup
      And, ignoring the mess,
      Pick the newspaper up,
      I settle me back,
      Put my cares on the shelf
      And take ten lovely minutes
      All to myself.

                Kay Andrew

All my life
I never really
thought of her as Mother
in the sense
that some people think
of a parent.
I thought of her more
as a great woman.

Pearl Bailey

Mother

In her the creative genius
of God attains its highest skill.
What a charming blend
she is of the most lovable and moving
qualities of human nature.
From the moment in youth when
she holds her first baby in her arms
until in life's evening time
she looks tenderly upon her grandchild,
her life is one of dedicated
service and love.
Loving us,
believing in us,
fighting for us,
praying for us,
to her we are always her dear child --
life of her life.

Norman Vincent Peale

A mother is all
those wonderful things
you never outgrow
your need for.

Kay Andrew

The many
make the household,
but only one
the home.

James Russell Lowell

Having a large family
is a more interesting experience
than any other that I know,
and it ought to be viewed
that way.
It's quite a challenge.

Rose Kennedy

A mother is not
a person to lean on,
but a person
to make leaning unnecessary.

Dorothy Canfield Fisher

All that I am
or hope to be,
I owe to my angel mother.

Abraham Lincoln

One of the most charming things
about Mother
was the extraordinary patience
with which she would allow
us youngsters
to ``instruct'' her.

Jean Kerr

24

My mother was the making of me.
She was so true,
so sure of me,
and I felt that I had
someone to live for;
someone I must not disappoint.

Thomas Edison

Whatever is good and true
    in my thoughts,
Whatever is beautiful
    and joyful in my spirit,
Whatever is courageous
    in my actions,
Whatever is faithful
    and understanding in my heart--
Are gifts
    from my wonderful mother.

Barbara Kunz Loots

A Gracious Lady

Her charm
   is not of worldly style;
There is a light
   about her face,
Reflected in her gentle smile,
Her air
   of sweetness and of grace.
Her patience
   under life's duress
Comes from her spirit's
   inner glow
That clothes her
   with a loveliness
Dependent not on outward show.

Kay Wissinger

Blessed be the hand
that prepares a pleasure
for a child,
for there is no saying
when and where
it may bloom forth.

Douglas Jerrold

When God thought of mother,
He must have laughed
with satisfaction
and framed it quickly--
so rich, so deep, so divine,
so full of soul, power,
and beauty
was the conception.

Henry Ward Beecher

...My Mama was really alert.
She seemed to know
every second
where I was,
what I was up to
and who I was with.
She had a seventh sense
and seemed to know
if I was just planning
to do something that was
out of order,
and that always gave
me pause to think--
and if we pause to think
we usually come up with
the right decision.

Pat Boone

For when you looked
into my mother's eyes
you knew,
as if He had told you,
why God sent her
into the world--
it was to open the minds
of all who looked,
to beautiful thoughts.

James M. Barrie

Mothers Are Wonderful

Mothers should know everything,
　　Like just how high is "up,"
How to kiss away a hurt
　　Or how to wash a pup;
Mothers should know everything,
　　Like how to mend old toys,
And how to tell a story
　　That delights small girls and boys;
Mothers should know everything,
　　Like how to fly a kite,
What makes a budding flower bloom,
　　Why stars come out at night;
Mothers should know everything--
　　(Even why the sky is blue!)
Yes, mothers should know everything--
　　And the wonder is--they DO!

　　　　　　Mary Dawson Hughes

Beautiful, the earth around her--
peaceful, the sky above,
Harmony and joy surround her--
gentle is a mother's love.

Ed Cunningham

I attribute my success
in life to the moral,
intellectual
and physical education
which I received
from my mother.

George Washington

... I have
an utterly fantastic relationship
with my kids - -
I'm their mother.

Phyllis Diller

The seasons come
And the seasons go
And many the changes they bring,
But in the warmth
Of a mother's heart,
It is forever spring.

Barbara Burrow

Youth fades; love droops;
    the leaves of friendship fall;
A mother's secret love
    outlives them all.

Oliver Wendell Holmes

Mothers give children
a goal to work toward,
an example to follow...
something that gold and silver
cannot buy.

Billy Graham

A mother is the only person
on earth
who can divide her love
among ten children
and each child still have
all her love.

Author Unknown

I occupy myself...
still enveloped in thoughts
of my dear Mother,
the most perfect
and magnetic character,
the rarest combination
of practical, moral and spiritual,
and the least selfish,
of all and any
I have ever known - -
and by me O so much
the most deeply loved.

from The Letters of Walt Whitman

Mother

... The angels,
whispering to one another,
Can find,
among their burning terms of love,
None so devotional
as that of "Mother" ....

Edgar Allan Poe

You may have friends--
fond, dear friends;
but never will you have again
the inexpressible love
and gentleness
lavished upon you
which none
but a mother bestows.

Thomas Babington Macaulay

Because she is
My Mother,
I so well understand
Why flowers bloom
Beneath the touch
Of her gentle hand.

Mary Rita Hurley

I was always glad
that I was a girl.
As a girl, I knew that someday
I would have children.
My closest models,
my mother and my grandmother,
had had both children
and a career.
So I had no doubt
that whatever career
I might choose,
I would have children too.

Margaret Mead

The Picture

The painter has
with his brush transferred
the landscape to the canvas
with such fidelity that the trees
and grasses seem almost real;
he has made
even the face of a maiden
seem instinct with life,
but there is one picture
so beautiful that no painter
has ever been able perfectly
to reproduce it,
and that is the picture
of the mother holding
in her arms her babe.

William Jennings Bryan

The Gift of Love

As long ago
    I carried to your knees
The tales and treasures
    of eventful days,
Knowing no deed too humble
    for your praise,
Nor any gift
    too trivial to please,
So still I bring,
    with older smiles and tears,
What gifts I may
    to claim the old, dear right:
Your faith beyond the silence
    and the night--
Your love still close
    and watching
        through the years.

John Grey

Though distance may come
between a mother and her child,
the bond that holds them close
will never weaken - -
the love they share
will never be more
than a memory apart.

Dean Walley

Set in Bernhard Fashion,
designed by Lucian Bernhard
for American Typefounders, 1929.
Printed on Hallmark Eggshell Book paper.
Designed by Myron McVay.